Acadia's Carriage Roads

A passage into the heart of the national park

To the memory of my brother John, whose
smile and gentle manner found a pathway
into the hearts of those who knew him.

Acadia's Carriage Roads

A passage into the heart of the national park

Written and Photographed by Robert A. Thayer

Down East Books • Camden, Maine

Copyright © 2002 Robert A. Thayer

ISBN 0-89272-551-6

Designed by Lindy Gifford

Cover photograph: *Cliffside Bridge and its crenellations make a difficult mountainside passable.*
Title page photograph: *Granite bedrock forms an outcropping near Witch Hole Pond.*
Back cover photograph: *The road leading up Day Mountain is resplendent in its autumn colors.*

5   4

Printed in China

Down East Books
P.O. Box 679
Camden, ME 04843
For book orders and catalog information, call 1-800-685-7962,
or visit our website at www.downeastbooks.com

The sun rises over Witch Hole Pond.

Contents

Preface

The creation of this book actually began in the summer of 1982, my first season as a naturalist at Acadia National Park. It was then that I discovered the carriage roads and set out to walk or bike all fifty-plus miles of them and to find all sixteen bridges. Although I accomplished my goal that summer, I also realized that the carriage roads could not be fully appreciated in a single season. Twenty years later, having written this book, I am still discovering new things about the roads, the bridges, and the people who built them.

In 1982 I had a ten-speed bicycle with narrow tires—not well suited for riding on roads that were badly eroded and often overgrown with vegetation. In the years that followed, the increased popularity of mountain bikes, combined with a restoration project, made the roads more comfortable to travel and more accessible to a greater number of people.

The photographs in this book span this twenty-year time frame. They reflect the many changes that have occurred in the past two decades. The roads, bridges, and vistas are now closer to their original condition, but some of my photographs may reflect their state before restoration began.

Along with human intervention, the forces of fires and storms periodically changed the natural scene along the carriage roads. For example, I originally wrote a section on Gilmore Meadow describing it as an open, grassy area near Aunt Betty's Pond. On a later visit, I discovered that a beaver community had transformed it into a shallow pond. Five years after the publication of this book, the beavers may be gone, and the meadow may have returned. Thus is the pattern of natural systems and the problem with photographs that can only capture a moment in time.

However transformed over the years, the carriage roads continue to serve as the easiest way to discover the inner beauty of Acadia.

Acknowledgments

Thank you to all who have contributed their time and knowledge to making this book a fitting tribute to the carriage roads and to the ideals of their creator. They include:

Michele Hiltzik–Archivist, Rockefeller Archive Center
Keith Miller–Superintendent of Acadia National Park from 1971 to 1978
Ken Olsen–President, Friends of Acadia
Debbie Dyer–Bar Harbor Historical Society
Brooke Childry–Archivist, National Park Service
Tom Vining–National Park Service
Steven Haynes–for his great stories of the quarrying activities on Mount Desert Island
Bryant Woods, Michael Furnari, and Linda Thayer for their editorial direction.
Willie Granston–The Great Harbor Maritime Museum, Northeast Harbor
All the people at Down East Books for their confidence and support, especially my editor, Chris Cornell, and designer, Lindy Gifford, who in the end complete the process and make my ideas come to life.

A special thanks to the Historic American Engineering Record (HAER), whose artwork graces this book and the others in my Acadia series. A group of talented artists and historians employed by the National Park Service, the HAER staff members document historically significant engineering works in the United States. Their drawings are not merely impressions of the bridges and buildings but accurate renderings. Each stone is as it occurs in real life. Acadia's bridges and buildings were recorded in 1994–1995, and the team members included: Todd Croteau, Richard Quin, David Haney, harlen d. Groe, Ed Lupyak, Sarah F. Desbiens, J. Shannon Barras, Kate E. Curtis, Joseph Korzenewski, and Neil Maher.

I had been walking for only a few minutes but could already feel the pressure of civilization being left behind. With each turn, the carriage road took me farther from the complex world of human discord, into one of simple, natural harmony. The contrast was striking and compelling.

I noticed a change in the air. Summer dust was replaced by the cool smell of balsam and spruce. Where the forest canopy opened, I paused to admire a rounded mountain mirrored in a small, glassy pond. The forest floor glowed with a myriad of lichens and mosses, and colorful flowers created highlights against a tapestry of green. The sense of unity and serenity was comforting, and I felt at peace.

I had gone for a simple walk in the woods and discovered instead a pathway to renew my spirit.

The creator of Acadia's carriage roads, John D. Rockefeller Jr., envisioned this type of experience when he built the carriage-road system on Mount Desert Island as an escape from the growing turmoil of city life. In the early twentieth century, Rockefeller was ahead of his time, for his roads were created just as America was beginning its love affair with the automobile. Time and the preservation afforded by the national park have allowed John Jr.'s creation to remain intact and to be fully appreciated in the twenty-first century.

The intent of this book is to explore the natural beauty revealed by the carriage roads and to show how creative engineering has provided a gentle pathway into the heart of Acadia National Park.

Hikers stop to admire the view along the Amphitheater Road.

John D. Rockefeller Jr.

John D. Rockefeller Jr. in his forties (circa 1915).

Acadia is unique among national parks in that it was established with the gifts of private donors, rather than by the preservation of public lands. In 1901 Charles Eliot, the president of Harvard College; George Dorr; and other summer residents of Mount Desert Island formed the Hancock County Trustees of Public Reservation. Their mission was to "acquire by devise, gift or purchase, and to own, arrange, hold, maintain or improve for public use land in Hancock County, Maine…" In 1903, two small parcels of land were given to the trustees, and in 1908 came its first substantial acquisition: the Bowl and the Beehive, a small pond and mountain near Sand Beach.

That same year, John D. Rockefeller Jr.; his wife, Abbey; and their two children vacationed in Bar Harbor. Abbey was expecting their third child (Nelson), who was born that August. The memories of that summer were so pleasant that the next year the Rockefellers rented again. Eventually, they purchased property in nearby Seal Harbor, where they built a large estate, the Eyrie. This was the beginning of a lifelong relationship with Mount Desert Island and Acadia National Park.

The fifth child and only son of John D. Rockefeller Sr., founder of Standard Oil Company, John Jr. was the heir to one of America's greatest fortunes and would make the Rockefeller name synonymous with philanthropy. Although the privilege of the family's wealth was obvious to others, it was less a factor in young John's upbringing than were the strong work ethic of his father and the devout religious attitudes of both his parents. In 1941, John Jr. presented a statement of principles under the title "I Believe," which reflect the tenets of his upbringing and the philosophy by which he lived his life. The construction of the carriage-road system and Rockefeller's giving it to Acadia National Park, personify this philosophy.

"I believe that every right implies a responsibility; every opportunity, an obligation; every possession, a duty."

Throughout his youth, John Jr. summered at the family estate in Forest Hill, west of Cleveland, Ohio, where his attitudes about life and his love of nature took shape. It was there and at Pocantico Hills, on the Hudson River in New York state, that he also learned how roads and paths could best be designed to heighten the experience of nature.

John Jr. shared a love of horses and carriage-driving with his father and was considered an excellent horseman. Tom Pyle, an employee at Pocantico Hills, wrote, "With the four-in-hand he was actually better than either the estate coachman or the head of the stable." Even when the automobile came into vogue, Rockefeller preferred to drive his carriage to work each day and was often seen "coaching" with his family in New York's Central Park.

The pressure of assuming the reins of his father's empire was a daunting task. John Jr. was an astute businessman, but in 1910, at the age of thirty-six, he decided to change his role in the family company. He would devote his energies to philanthropy, directing his wealth to the betterment of society. The scope of his subsequent endeavors would encompass religion, education, health, and conservation. He showed a special interest in historic preservation and in the formation and development of national parks.

"I believe that the rendering of useful service is the common duty of mankind and that only in the purifying fire of sacrifice is the dross of selfishness consumed and the greatness of the human soul set free."

John D. Rockefeller Jr.'s love of nature and his abilities as a landscape designer converged in the building of the carriage-road system on Mount Desert Island. He envisioned a network of roads stretching from one side of the island to the other, connecting the major populated areas and opening the interior to the public. He quietly began purchasing land with this mission in mind. Rockefeller was particular about the projects he undertook. He wanted to expend his efforts on fresh, undisturbed areas. Mount Desert Island and the rapidly growing national-park movement provided just such an opportunity. His carriage roads would strike that delicate balance between preserving nature and providing access to those seeking a natural experience.

The automobile came late to Mount Desert Island. In 1907, the Maine state legislature passed a bill giving individual towns the right to ban or permit cars. By 1913, automobiles were allowed in some towns on the island, but not in the town of Mount Desert (which includes Otter Creek, Northeast and Seal Harbors, Somesville, and Pretty Marsh). This severely restricted vehicular traffic on the island and was a source of concern and controversy among local and seasonal residents. A poem by Herbert Weir Smythe recounts the events of the Mount Desert town meeting where a vote took place on eliminating the prohibition on automobiles.

Now, glory hallelujah, hip, hip and three times
*   three,*
Mount Desert town, of fair renown from autos
*   will be free.*
In Eden Town they rage around, with horrid smell
*   and soot,*
And make Bar Harbor's streets unsafe for those
*   who go afoot;*
But Northeast and Seal Harbors are in Mount
*   Desert Town,*
And the autos in town meeting, have there been
*   voted down.*

The poem goes on to explain how one after another, wealthy summer residents, including John D. Rockefeller Jr., rose and pleaded to continue the ban and maintain the quiet charm of island life. They were successful, and the town overwhelmingly voted in favor of the status quo. While this act slowed the wheels of progress, they could not be stopped. Two years later the state legislature, influenced by the auto industry and the other towns on the island, passed a resolution *requiring* the town of Mount Desert to allow automobiles on its roads. In that same year, Rockefeller began in earnest the task of expanding the carriage-road system that he had started in 1913. His hope was to preserve forever the natural serenity that existed before the automobile.

Road Construction

"I believe in the dignity of labor, whether with head or hand; that the world owes no man a living but that it owes every man an opportunity to make a living."

As functional as they are, Acadia's carriage roads are the product of a past era. Constructed with the lay of the land, they rarely follow a straight path. The traveler's eye is drawn into the forest or to an open view, not to the road itself. These byways are built for touring, not for speed. The journey is the destination and the road simply a vehicle of presentation.

Local engineer Charles P. Simpson was hired to oversee the entire construction project. When Charles became ill in 1921, his son, Paul D. Simpson, continued the job. In later years, Walters G. Hill, another local contractor, also played a major role, as did S. F. Ralston, Rockefeller's superintendent at the Eyrie.

The carriage roads are not simple dirt trails or paths, but rather broken-stone roads built to the highest standards of the day. Referred to by Rockefeller as "rock-filled roads," they were constructed with three layers of progressively smaller stones: a foundation, middle tier, and finished surface. This top layer consisted of crushed rock that was mixed with a clay binder and pressed wet with a two-ton roller, creating a hard, nearly impervious surface that withstood erosion and made for smooth riding.

Great care was taken to provide the roads with adequate drainage, for this in the long run would

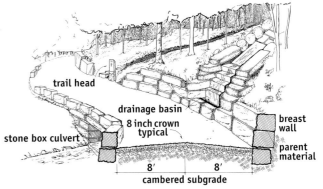

TYPICAL LANDSCAPE ELEMENTS

L. T. MOORE

A carriage rider takes in the view from the overlook above Little Long Pond (from an early postcard).

A derrick eases the backbreaking labor of moving stones.

considered to be bridle paths, not carriage roads.)

Rockefeller was adamant that every effort be taken to minimize the disturbance to the surrounding landscape, and he insisted that when each section of road was completed, the area be restored to a natural appearance. In woodlands, where cuts were necessary, breast walls above the road and retaining walls below were constructed to allow a much "narrower path of disturbance." Coping stones, often referred to as "Rockefeller's teeth," were placed as natural barriers on sharp curves and steep roadsides. The design specifications stipulated that they were "not to be in a line, but at irregular angles to create a rustic appearance."

At road intersections, triangular islands of trees were often created to provide a gentle change of direction and to mask the expanse of roadway that the intersection required. The islands also provided a logical point for travelers to stop and consider the best route to their destination.

Good drainage is important to maintaining stone roads.

reduce maintenance. Each had a center crown eight inches higher than its edges and was flanked by two-foot-wide "gutters" with enough depth to carry off the water. Culverts were built of stone where possible, and catch basins were put at the entrance of each culvert to hold debris and prevent it from blocking the flow of water.

Most gravel roads of the day were not pre-planned but rather constructed from the experience of the crew at the site. Rockefeller's roads, however, were carefully designed on paper to ensure "a beautiful, flowing line in the landscape." Virtually all were built sixteen feet wide to provide ample room for two carriages to pass. (Some sections, however, are only ten feet wide and are

Still, much of the road construction was done by hand.

Although the landscape surrounding the roads was to appear natural, that did not mean untouched to Rockefeller. He believed that the roadsides should be cleared of brush and downed trees, creating a more orderly, "park-like" scene. Rockefeller himself made the final decisions on landscape design, but he would usually defer to the engineers at the site on technical matters. As the roads began to expand and time limited his involvement, he sought the advice of noted landscape architect Beatrix Farrand, a longtime summer resident of Bar Harbor. Rockefeller and his engineers designed the roads to take advantage of scenic vistas and other points of interest on the island, but it was Farrand who recommended the actual plantings along the roadsides, bridges, and gate lodges.

She would travel the carriage roads often, making copious notes on plants that would add interest to the roadsides and cover the scars of construction. Her notes also included recommendations for *removing* vegetation, especially sprouts that would eventually grow to block a view. Because of the relatively mild climate of the island, Beatrix Farrand had a broad selection of plants from which to choose, but she preferred using native tree species—pine, spruce, maple, or birch—and

Islands of trees create natural intersections.

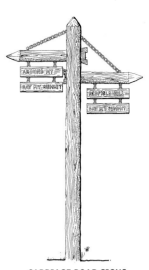

CARRIAGE ROAD SIGNS

Coping stones along the roadside provide assurance on steep embankments.

Breast walls minimize the impact a road has on the landscape.

11

shrubs such as bayberry, winterberry, and sweet fern, to name but a few.

John D. Rockefeller Jr. had a passion for building roads and was a perfectionist about the details of their construction. But this was not the indulgence of a wealthy man's hobby. These roads were built to accomplish the greater goal of providing access to the inner reaches of the island. Time and nature have healed the scars of construction, leaving today only the beauty that the roads were meant to reveal.

Until his death in 1960, Rockefeller assumed the responsibility of maintaining the carriage roads, even though most of them were by then in the national park. He employed a crew dedicated to clearing vegetation from gutters and culverts, keeping vistas and roadsides open, and performing maintenance on buildings and bridges. After his death, the job fell to the park service, whose budget and staff were not sufficient to keep the car-riage roads in their original condition. By the 1980s, the years of neglect were becoming obvious. Surface coats were gone, crowns lost, culverts and basins filled with debris—all allowing erosion to literally wash the roads away. Vistas created by the vision of Beatrix Ferrand were now obscured. Concurrently, interest in the carriage roads was increasing as park visitation grew and more people were seeking to experience all aspects of Acadia.

In 1991, the Friends of Acadia, a fund-raising and watchdog organization, spearheaded an effort to restore the ailing carriage-road system. In a historic agreement, the federal government agreed to match the private contributions raised by the Friends. Each party contributed four million dollars, which guarantees that the carriage roads will be maintained in perpetuity and ensure that John D. Rockefeller Jr.'s vision will continue to inspire and educate future generations.

Hemlock Bridge was built in 1928.

Beatrix Farrand in her Bar Harbor garden.

Each bridge took about a year to construct. (This is Duck Brook Bridge, circa 1924.)

12

Bridge Construction

Acadia's carriage-road system includes seventeen stone bridges: Sixteen were built by Rockefeller, and the seventeenth, crossing the Park Loop Road near Wildwood Stables, was built by the park service in 1941.

These bridges are more than just a means of connecting two points; they are handcrafted works of art executed by highly skilled masons. Each one followed the "standards of excellence" laid out in Henry G. Tyrell's *Artistic Bridge Design*, which decreed that a bridge should conform to its environment and be appropriate for its site; that it be constructed simply, with an economic use of materials; and that it not be overly ornamented. Tyrell states, "A spectator is more impressed by the general form than by an endless wealth of details, and when the outline is correct, little detail ornament is needed." Rockefeller wanted the bridges to be rustic and irregular, and he sometimes admonished the masons for making them too "neat, true and fine."

The bridges were designed by noted architects Wells Boswell (working from 1917 to 1929) and Charles Stoughton (working from 1929 to 1933). Rockefeller was a participant in every design detail and was frequently consulted during construction. Whenever possible, he wanted the granite to be quarried at or near the site so that its appearance would match the local bedrock and so that the cost of transportation would be minimized. When a bridge was completed, the small quarry would be relandscaped to cover any scars. In some cases, Rockefeller directed that designs be changed or routes modified to better fit the landscape or to preserve vegetation or an important geologic feature. He was in continuous contact with his engineers and knew many of the workers by name.

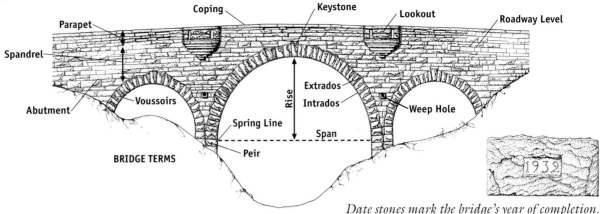

BRIDGE TERMS

Date stones mark the bridge's year of completion.

In an article written for *Down East* magazine in 1982, Victor Layton, then the harbormaster of Northeast Harbor, described the typical day of a mason working on the carriage-road bridges.

"Early morning, before sunrise, these craftsmen converged on Acadia by foot, bicycle, or car, following the partially built carriage roads to the bridge construction sites for the beginning of the workday at seven. They normally worked eight hours with a thirty-minute lunch break, which they took at the smithy, where their home-prepared pail lunches were kept warm near the forge."

The stones were rough-cut at the quarry, usually a short distance from the bridge, then transported to the construction site and placed on a motorized, circular cutting platform. Here the masons would shape them to the required dimensions. "One well-shaped, good-sized stone per man, per day was considered an acceptable average," wrote Layton.

"The abrasive stone dust was hard on clothing, and the men wore aprons made from inexpensive mattress ticking for protection, but the penetrating dust wore out everything . . ." The construction sites were noisy, dusty, and potentially hazardous places to work ". . . and there is no indication that the cutters ever used safety glasses, hard hats, or steel-toed shoes. The daily pay for a qualified stonecutter started at $5.00 in the early twenties, rising to about $10.50 by 1933." This was a good wage, considering that the time frame for the building of the carriage roads and bridges coincided with the Depression. Undoubtedly, all of those employed by Rockefeller were thankful for the opportunity to work.

Calcium carbonate forms as water leaches the minerals from the mortar.

13

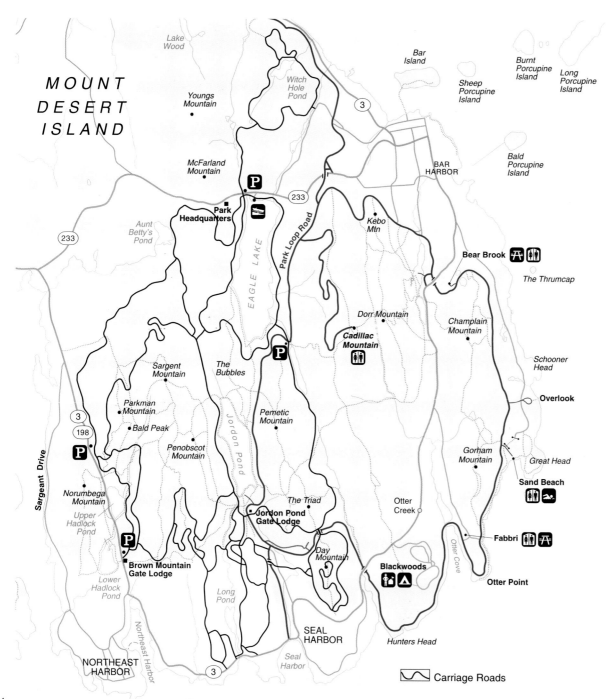

MOUNT DESERT ISLAND

Carriage Road Tours

The carriage roads of Acadia National Park all interconnect. For organizational purposes they are presented here in manageable sections, or tours. In the park, wherever the carriage roads converge, signs point to possible destinations. Each signpost has a wooden number, put there in the mid 1980s, and these can be used to pinpoint your location. Where appropriate those numbers are included.

The directions in this book are not meant to be a definitive guide but rather a means to get you started on your own journey of discovery into the heart of Acadia.

From the town of Seal Harbor, the motor road enters Acadia National Park by following a small meandering brook through a pristine spruce-and-fir forest. After crossing the brook a number of times, the road passes beneath the center span of the impressive, triple-arched **Stanley Brook Bridge**, a fitting introduction to Acadia's carriage-road system. The arch on the left crosses the seaside path from Seal Harbor to Jordan Pond; Stanley Brook flows beneath the arch on the right. Above is the carriage road that leads from Day Mountain to the Jordan Pond sections of the road system.

Built in 1933, the Stanley Brook Bridge was the last of Rockefeller's sixteen bridges, and it reflects the accumulated experience of twenty-five years of construction. The bridge was designed by Charles Stoughton and built by S. F. Ralston. Each of the arches is faced with granite, and the sides have an interesting mixture of large "quarry-faced" (rough-finished) blocks combined with smaller pieces of granite and occasional cobblestones. The upper deck has fine-tooled railings (parapets) that rise to a peak at the center and flare with the road at the approaches. On three sides, each parapet ends with an elaborate stone

The Stanley Brook Bridge is a beautiful introduction to the carriage-road system.

STANLEY BROOK BRIDGE

The stonework of this bridge varies from large cut blocks to small cobblestones.

The Seaside Path passes beneath one of the three arches.

edifice, while on the fourth side is a viewing platform. Much of the bridge's landscaping can still be identified as that selected by Beatrix Farrand.

In the fall of 2000, Stanley Brook Bridge was the first bridge to be restored as part of the Friends of Acadia preservation project that had so improved the roads. The beauty of the stone and the natural flow of the bridge's design are once again revealed as they appeared in 1933.

Shortly after the Stanley Brook Bridge, the motor road merges with the Park Loop Road, which leads to the Jordan Pond House.

Technically a lake, Jordan Pond is the strategic hub of the southern half of the carriage-road system and is the starting point for the first five tours described here. In the early days, the Jordan Pond House restaurant was a favorite destination for

hikers and carriage riders, either for lunch or afternoon tea. Today it serves the same purpose, but many more visitors now arrive by automobile. Parking is limited at the restaurant, but more is available just down the road, adjacent to the boat ramp. From the ramp, follow the path to the left, around the southern end of the pond, and onto the carriage road. Before beginning the journey, take a moment to admire the view across the pond, where you'll see the rounded peaks of North Bubble and South Bubble.

Jordan Pond was created twelve thousand years ago as the glaciers retreated. The U-shaped valley and the rounded landscape are evidence of their effect. At the pond's southern end, the restaurant sits on a glacial moraine, which blocks the water's flow to the ocean. This created the lake, whose outlet—Jordan Stream—cuts through this moraine, exposing boulders left by the glacier. The first tour follows the path of Jordan Stream as it makes its way through the forest to the sea.

Jordan Pond is the southern hub of the carriage-road system.

Jordan Pond to Little Long Pond

At the end of the lake, Jordan Stream spills over a dam and passes beneath the Jordan Pond Dam Bridge. This is one of several small bridges modeled after similar structures that Rockefeller admired in New York City's Central Park.

Follow the carriage road to the left of the bridge, and bear right at the next intersection (15). A relatively steep and narrow bridle path meanders across the stream and provides an interesting alternative to the carriage road. The open, wooded forest through which it passes is often cool and moist on warm summer days. Within less than a mile, the path returns to the carriage road (23), which in a short distance crosses the Cobblestone Bridge (24). Note that the bridge and the road beyond this point are privately owned but are open to the public. Bicycles, however, are not allowed on this section of the carriage road.

The **Cobblestone Bridge** was the first major structure built as part of the carriage-road system. William Welles Bosworth, a well-known New York architect who had previously done work for Rockefeller, designed it. Charles Simpson, Rockefeller's local engineer, suggested the use of cobblestones to face the sides and line the "barrel" (exposed underside) of the bridge. Simpson felt that this feature would help the span to better fit the surroundings and blend with the boulders in the stream. Rockefeller agreed. The moss-faced stones were placed on a wooden form, with the larger ends up (to prevent them from falling when the forms were removed). Then, steel-reinforced concrete was poured over the stones to cement them in place. An addendum to the contract for this bridge suggests that "picturesque freedom may be followed in the stonework…"

Although each bridge in the system is different, Cobblestone stands alone as the only one not con-

A bridle path follows Jordan Stream.

COBBLESTONE BRIDGE

structed of cut stone. Subsequent bridges were all made from quarried granite, as a ready supply of cobblestones was unavailable. Not everyone shared Simpson's and Rockefeller's enthusiasm for the design. George Dorr, then the superintendent of the park, commented: "... all have agreed in regretting it from the artistic standpoint, but vegetation now is closing in around it, and it will soon be little noticeable." Today this bridge's uniqueness makes it one of the most photographed and loved structures in the park.

From this point, the carriage road continues to follow the stream for a short distance. At the first intersection (28), bear to the right as the road descends to the sea. Here it skirts an open meadow with views of Little Long Pond. This is the southern end of the carriage-road system, and from this vantage there is a spectacular view of the pond and the mountains at the end of the valley. Charles Eliot considered this to be "the most beautiful view on the island."

The Cobblestone Bridge is one of the most photographed because of its unique stonework.

Charles Eliot considered this to be "the most beautiful view on the island."

Jordan Pond to Day Mountain

*The next tour begins at the **Jordan Pond Gate Lodge**, across the street from the Jordan Pond House restaurant. Before moving on, take a moment to view the lodge, which now serves as housing for park personnel and is not open to the public.*

Grosvenor Atterbury, the designer of the gate lodges, was keenly aware of the daunting task of building a man-made structure in a national park so that it did not intrude on the natural experience. In a report completed after a research visit to other national parks he wrote: *"… any architecture in our national parks is bound to be, in fact, the physical point of contact, comparison, and contrast between the latest handiwork of human civilization and the oldest untouched monuments of Nature. The handiwork of man in the face of the work of God."*

The gate-lodge complexes at Jordan Pond and Brown Mountain were built in the French Romanesque style, inspired by the striped architecture of the Le Puis district in France. The first floor of the Jordan Pond house is faced with alternating granite blocks and narrow bands of "seamfaced" granite (stone that was split rather than cut). This design is continuous throughout the attached carriage house, low wall, and small gate towers. The overhanging second floor, with its three hipped-roof-dormer windows, is half-timbered with red brick infill. The steeply pitched roof, large end chimneys, and casement windows all give the building an appearance that naturally belongs in a national park.

Here, too, Beatrix Farrand was called upon to do the landscaping. Both she and Rockefeller agreed that the plantings should be native so that the building would blend with its surroundings.

The *Historic Resource Study of the Carriage Road System*, completed in 1989 by William

The gate lodges are comparisons "between the latest handiwork of human civilization and the oldest untouched monuments of Nature."

Beatrix Farrand surrounded the lodges with native plants.

The gates control access to the carriage roads.

Rieley, compares the gate lodge at Jordan Pond to those in Europe. "European gate lodges, after which this was modeled, served two functions: to welcome people to the grounds of the estate and to house the gatekeeper. It was a pretentious building with a humble function . . . it housed a working-class family in a structure that also served as a symbol of the owner's wealth, power, and taste." Acadia's gate lodges were also intended to serve a dual function: to control the flow of traffic onto the carriage roads and to house a gatekeeper.

In this case, no such person was ever employed. Charles P. Simpson, Rockefeller's engineer, and his family lived in the house at Jordan Pond until 1941. Although picturesque, it was apparently drafty and difficult to heat. After one cold winter, Simpson moved his family to their home in Seal Harbor and lived in the gate lodge only in the summer. It was deeded to the park in 1939.

The completion of Acadia's gate lodges was hailed with much fanfare and adoration. In 1932 Rockefeller wrote to Atterbury: "The two gate lodges are the talk of the entire state. People come from all about to see and photograph them.... Mr. Graves, the contractor, simply adores both the buildings and talks about them as though they were his favorite sons." Later, Atterbury wrote to Rockefeller about comments he had received on one of the gate lodges: "When I met Secretary [of the Interior] Ickes lately, he told me that he intended to make application as caretaker so as to live in it after he retires from public service."

Pass through the gates and onto the carriage road. For a distance, it winds through a low, often wet forest then slowly climbs the side of the Triad just above Wildwood Stables. Here the road passes a large granite cliff face, a good place to stop and study the stone that is the bedrock of Mount Desert Island.

Granite walls still bear the signs of road construction.

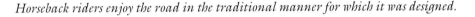

Horseback riders enjoy the road in the traditional manner for which it was designed.

It is no accident that the bridges, the gate lodges, and the carriage roads themselves are all made of local granite, for it is of this stone that most of Mount Desert Island is composed. At nearly every turn and hillside, the road reveals outcroppings of this beautiful, pink-toned rock.

Some four hundred million years ago, a giant magma chamber existed beneath this spot. The surface above it experienced volcanic activity, but the magma below would cool and harden several miles within the earth. Slowly, crystals of quartz, hornblende, and feldspar grew large and formed the rock we know as granite. Over many millions of years, erosion has removed the overlying earth, exposing the resistant granites that are the mountains of Acadia.

Not all of the granite cooled at the same rate nor contained the same minerals. In his 1988 survey of the geology of Mount Desert Island, Richard Gilman identified ten different types of granite, each with a distinctive color and crystal

21

Meadowsweet

Steeplebush

Flannel mullein

Blackberry

Dogbane

Butter-and-eggs

size. It was for this reason that the stone for each bridge was quarried near its construction site—to match the structure with its surroundings.

On this cliff face, and on nearly every exposed ledge along the carriage road, can be found signs of construction. Drill holes running down the face of the stone indicate where small half-rounds and wedges were placed in a row and slowly hammered until the granite began to crack and eventually split. (Learning the "rift and grain" of such stone took years of experience.)

If a piece of quarried granite was to be used for a bridge or gate lodge, it would then have been worked with a side hammer to remove these holes. Coping stones and granite ledges still bear the scars of this process and tell the story of the road builders' efforts.

Mount Desert Island granite was prized as a building material for its hard composition and unique colors. Quarrying was a major industry here, beginning around 1870, seeing its heyday in the early 1880s, and ending in the 1920s. At the turn of the century, the island undoubtedly looked very different than it does today. Extensive lumbering in the 1800s had cleared the landscape, exposing the granite bedrock. That, in turn, promoted quarrying of the valuable stone. Steven Haynes, a local resident researching the granite industry, estimates that there were once more than sixty quarries on Mount Desert Island.

Nearly all of the stone was shipped out of the state by schooner, to become buildings in New York, Philadelphia, and Washington D.C. Acadia's bridges and gate lodges represent one of the few examples where Mount Desert Island granite was used as a building material in Maine.

At intersection 17, the road forks three ways. Continuing straight leads you to Bubble Pond. Take a sharp right, almost doubling back, and you'll descend a steep hill to the Wildwood riding stables. Making a full ninety-degree right-hand turn leads you across the Park Loop Road on the Triad-Day Mountain Bridge, and that is the route to take for this tour. This bridge was built by the park service in 1941 as part of the loop road, and it only coincidentally connected the Jordan Pond and Day Mountain sections of the carriage-road system. After crossing the bridge, go in either direction to circle the mountain. At intersection 38, a spur winds to the summit of Day Mountain.

At several points along this summit road, the canopy opens to reveal views of distant landscapes and the ocean beyond. These clearings also create a unique habitat between the open, rocky road and the cool, shaded forest. Poor soil and harsh lighting are demanding conditions placed upon the organisms that make this location their home. Strangely, the diversity of life is often increased in such habitat by what ecologists call the "edge effect"—a condition where two environments meet and where there are representatives from each, along with organisms that only exist in the edge. The borders of the carriage roads are just such a place and are rich with the plants and animals of both open roadsides and shaded woodlands.

The **Day Mountain Road** is an ideal location to find many of these sun-loving plants. It was the last road in the system to be built and is the only one that goes to a summit. Although the peak's elevation is a mere 583 feet, it nonetheless provides excellent views of coastal islands and the mountains to the north and west.

The Cranberry Islands look spectacular from Day Mountain.

Fog can limit the view of Bubble Pond.

Jordan Pond to Bubble Pond

This tour begins as did the previous one: From Jordan Pond Gate Lodge, proceed to intersection 17. Continue straight toward Bubble Pond. The road winds through the wooded valley between Cadillac and Pemetic Mountains, ending at Bubble Pond Bridge.

Fog is a frequent visitor to Mount Desert Island. Its cool, wet blanket provides an ideal climate for the ferns, mosses, and evergreens that inhabit the exposed coastal forest. Created where the warm waters of the Gulf Stream meet the cold Labrador Current, fog creeps onto the land when the wind direction is favorable.

Fog may limit the view, but it is not a deterrent for enjoying the carriage roads. Protected beneath a canopy of trees, the traveler can walk the well-drained roads with dry and secure footing. The fog's thick, gray shroud creates an air of mystery as the road winds to some unseen distant point.

With the long view obscured, your eye is drawn to the nearer beauty along the roadside. The leaves glow with brilliant greens against wet, dark tree trunks. Spider webs, laden with moisture, sparkle in an otherwise muted scene. The smell of balsam and spruce fills the air, along with the sound of a distant foghorn and perhaps the call of a loon. In fact, venturing into the fog could reveal the true beauty that the carriage roads have to offer.

Bubble Pond sits in the bottom of a narrow, U-shaped valley, flanked on both sides by steep mountain walls. Like most of the bodies of water on the island, it is a product of glacial action. Today, Bubble Pond is quite different than it was in the cold and sterile years of its youth.

Where the water meets the shore, the pond is shallow and rocky. Fish cannot swim and trees cannot grow. Here is another edge environment that is neither pond nor land. Growing in undeveloped soil with continuously wet roots, only specialized plants can survive, species such as the water lobelia and the swamp horsetail.

Other varieties have found a unique solution to the mineral shortage—they eat insects. Small red patches clustered near the water's edge may be tiny sundew. This beautifully designed plant, its red spikes tipped with silver drops of "dew," is actually a trap for unsuspecting insects. Any contact with its sticky fluid and a small insect is hopelessly mired. Slowly the sundew then wraps around its prey and begins the process of digestion, providing the plant with needed nutrients.

The pitcher plant has a very different structure and approach to capturing its insect meals. With a long cylindrical body wound into the shape of a pitcher, it initially attracts prey with a red veiny outer lip. Once there, the insect is lured inside by an intoxicating odor. Tiny hairs lining the walls of the plant direct the prey downward, but when the hairs abruptly end, the insect slips into a pit of digestive juices at the bottom of the pitcher. Unable to escape, it becomes a meal for the pitcher plant.

In 1928, construction of this carriage road had reached the north end of Bubble Pond, where it intersected with the Park Loop Road. To separate the two byways, it was determined that a bridge would be needed. As with the previous eight bridges, Rockefeller gave the task to his architect, Welles Bosworth. Because this section of land was in the park, final approval for any construction went to Arno Cammerer, the park service director.

Bosworth's plans called for "a multicentered arch, finely cut stone work, and open balustrades." Cammerer, however, wrote to Rockefeller asking to have the plans changed to reflect a rustic appearance more appropriate for a national park. Bosworth's second concept still appeared too "citified" for Cammerer's taste, but he was somewhat uncomfortable placing more demands on the person who was funding the project. So, he had a third and final set of plans drawn by park-service architects Daniel Hull and Thomas Vint. Rockefeller reluctantly approved this third plan.

A Philadelphia mason, Pringle Bothwick, was hired to build the bridge. He changed the underlying construction by using all stone in lieu of the concrete core that is at the center of all the other carriage-road spans. Bothwick's costs were so reasonable that Rockefeller retained him to build the next bridge at Duck Brook.

Today, although the carriage road still crosses the bridge, the motor road no longer passes beneath it. In the 1940s the loop road was realigned and the bridge bypassed. In the 1980s, the park service planted trees on what was once the Park Loop Road.

BOSWORTH'S ORIGINAL PROPOSAL

BOSWORTH'S REVISED PROPOSAL

NATIONAL PARK SERVICE DESIGN

Horsetails thrive in the shallow, rocky shore of the pond.

The Pitcher Plant lures insects to its open mouth.

The Sundew is a small but effective insect trap.

Jordan Pond to Amphitheater Bridge

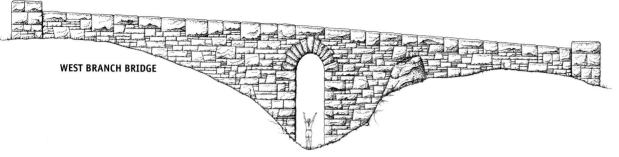

WEST BRANCH BRIDGE

The Amphitheater is a glacially carved valley lying between Cedar Swamp Mountain and Jordan Ridge. Accessible only by foot trail, it had always been considered a relatively wild section of the island. When John D. Rockefeller Jr. proposed extending his carriage roads into this "wilderness," most people were pleased, as this would provide a more direct route from Northeast Harbor to Jordan Pond. Others, however, questioned the road's impact on the area.

George W. Pepper, a summer resident of Northeast Harbor and a U.S. senator from Pennsylvania, was concerned that the carriage road would allow too much access and bring ruin to the park: "…we shall destroy the distinctive character of the Island and reduce the whole proposition to a dead level mediocrity. I should be sorry to have the whole thing degenerate into the Lafayette National Picnic Park with tin cans and eggs shells on the side." (Lafayette was the original name of the park before it was changed to Acadia in 1929.)

Pepper's concern was unfounded. He had undoubtedly seen and even used the existing carriage roads but was likely unaware of the great care that Rockefeller was taking to neither disturb the environment nor change the character of the area adjacent to each byway. Nonetheless, Rockefeller temporarily ceased construction on this section of the system. Ten years later, in the early thirties, however, the Amphitheater road was finally completed, including construction of three major bridges.

Again, begin at the southern end of Jordan Pond. Cross the bridge, and follow the carriage road for a tenth of a mile, taking a left at the next intersection (14) and heading toward the Amphitheater. In less than half a mile, the road makes a sharp bend over the West Branch Bridge and soon after that crosses the Cliffside Bridge.

West Branch Bridge has a narrow, six-foot-wide arch.

The **West Branch Bridge** crosses a branch of Jordan Stream. Like others in the system, it was modeled after a footbridge in New York City's Central Park. Its narrow, six-foot-wide arch symmetrically divides the curved 115-foot-long wall of cut stone. The bridge's roadway was made a full twenty feet wide (most of the carriage roads are sixteen) to allow carriages to easily navigate its sharp turn.

Another half-mile from the West Branch Bridge, a cliff face required the construction of a bridge (or half-arch) to make the area passable. Appropriately named the **Cliffside Bridge**, it runs for 230 feet along the south wall of Jordan Ridge. Massive upright stones create a crenellated parapet that gives the bridge the appearance of a large English castle, complete with towered viewing platforms and a commanding view of the countryside. Projecting from these platforms, elaborate chutes drain water from the road's surface. This bridge does not cross a stream or a road but rather is a creative solution to a difficult engineering problem.

During the construction at the cliff face, this section of the road was within the boundaries of the park, so decisions concerning the road involved park personnel. Being an avid hiker and outdoorsman, George Dorr, then Acadia's superintendent, reveled in the opportunity to survey the terrain and make suggestions. In a letter to Rockefeller, Dorr wrote: ". . . I have spent a great deal of time at the point and think the difficulty can be solved by making a direct, wide-angled approach to the shelf . . . and building an arch against the cliff. Such an arch . . . might be made a feature of interest and beauty and would leave the continuity of the cliff—itself a feature of great interest—as well as the climb unbroken." The unique architecture of the Cliffside Bridge certainly does create a "feature of interest" along this section of road, and its construction finally completed the Amphitheater loop that was started ten years earlier.

The crenellated parapets and towered viewing platforms of Cliffside Bridge create the image of an English castle.

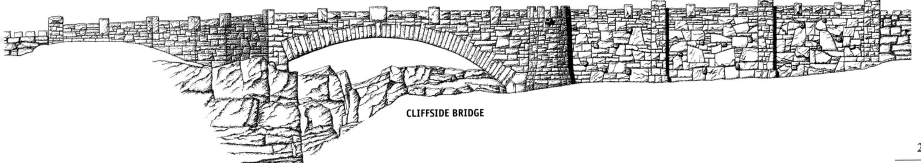

CLIFFSIDE BRIDGE

Rooting Collybia   Amanita

The dark, moist forest floor is alive with activity.

This section of the park has grown, undisturbed, for more than a hundred years, providing the visitor with an opportunity to examine the often-overlooked inhabitants of the floor of a mature conifer forest.

When Sarah Orne Jewett described the coast of Maine as "The Country of the Pointed Firs," she was undoubtedly looking up as evergreens created a skyline against the horizon of the open sea. But the view of those traveling the carriage roads is often drawn in the opposite direction, into the depths of the forest floor. Although less romantic than the pointed firs, the tangled roots and small plants there are major characters in an equally important story.

While the tops of the trees reach for light, their roots compete for water and minerals in the island's shallow, rocky soil. This is the world of mosses, ferns, and mushrooms—organisms whose role is to absorb water, make soil, and glean what little light they can through the dense evergreen canopy above.

Many fern species thrive in the low-light conditions of the forest floor. Hardy and diverse, they can be found in nearly any habitat. Each spring new plants emerge as delicate fiddleheads, which soon open into fanlike fronds. Although large in size, ferns have a relatively primitive means of reproduction: spores, rather than flowers. Each fern has a unique location for its spores. Some form clusters on the underside of the leaf, others may produce a separate stalk. Spore location is a key component of the plant's identity.

More common, but less prominent than the ferns, are the mosses, which also reproduce with spores. On close examination, stiff brown stalks can be seen emerging from the small, green plants. At the tip of every stalk, dangling like a lantern on a light pole, is a little case housing thousands of spores. When these are mature, a drop of rain or a passing animal may provide the stimulus that sends clouds of spores into the air, beginning the next cycle of the moss's life. Without a vascular system, mosses are relegated to the moist,

Fiddleheads

Indian Pipe

Haircap Moss spreads its spores.

Ferns, mosses, and flowering plants thrive here.

shaded environments on the forest floor, where they are never too far from the water they require to live and reproduce.

Beneath its benign surface, the soil hosts an intricate maze of microscopic life. The working cells of fungi are everywhere, absorbing and decomposing the twigs, needles, and leaves that have fallen from the plants and trees above. When conditions are right, these unorganized threads combine to produce temporary structures—mushrooms—

to elevate and disperse their spores. These are the only visible clues to the never-ending toil taking place beneath the surface.

Life on the forest floor is slow and methodical; it is a place where the grinding forces of geology meet the persistent drive of life. Often unappreciated, this struggle is essential to the trees that tower above.

Along with plants, the forest floor also hosts an array of animal life. Much of the park's wildlife is

elusive and seen only at dusk or dawn, but many smaller animals are less shy and more active during the day. Snakes, chipmunks, birds, and snowshoe hares are conspicuous as they busily look for food on the forest floor.

After leaving the Cliffside Bridge continue right at the next intersection (21) along the south wall of the amphitheater. At the end of the valley the road takes a sharp left turn over the Amphitheater Bridge.

Eastern garter snake

Chipmunk

Snowshoe (varying) hare

AMPHITHEATER BRIDGE

Amphitheater Bridge curves to cross the valley.

In the early spring or after a heavy rain, the little waterfall just upstream from the **Amphitheater Bridge** is noisy and white with foam. The stone structure was built with a view of the waterfall in mind, and it provides an example of the extraordinary steps that Rockefeller and his contractors routinely took to preserve the esthetics of the landscape.

In the proposed path of the bridge were two large trees—a twenty-foot-diameter pine and an equally large hemlock. The long span and sharp curve of the structure necessitated a width of twenty feet, as with the West Branch Bridge, but this meant either removing one of the trees or changing the location of the project, neither of which was acceptable to Rockefeller. The problem was solved with creative engineering. Paul Simpson explained: "By building the arch on a skew, the span could be somewhat reduced and the view of the stream toward the waterfall made a little more direct.... As there are few large trees at the site, however, it would be well to save both hemlock and pine if possible...." This was done, and the trees were saved along with the view of the falls. For nearly sixty years, these two trees served as sentinels guarding the curve of the bridge.

Today the pine tree is gone, as is the top of the hemlock, but the bridge and waterfall continue to serve as reminders that creative solutions can allow manmade structures to exist in harmony with a natural setting.

Jordan Pond to Parkman Mountain

This tour coincides with part of the "around the mountain" loop that many of the road signs indicate. The whole loop is an ambitious undertaking on foot or on a bicycle, being more than eleven miles long and quite steep in some sections. The road actually circles three mountains: Sargent, Penobscot, and Parkman. The entire loop is not presented here but can be completed by combining this tour with parts of the Hadlock and Amphitheater sections.

Begin the tour at Jordan Pond by crossing the Jordan Pond Dam Bridge and continuing straight at the next intersection (14). The road traverses an open woodland between Jordan Pond and Jordan Cliffs. In less than a mile, it rises through a large open boulder field, locally called the tumbledown.

Technically a talus slope, the tumbledown was created by a combination of glacial action, erosion, and gravity. When the glacier moved over this area, it dislodged these great blocks of granite from the side of Penobscot Mountain. As the ice melted, the side of the mountain collapsed to create the boulder field and the dramatic cliff face above it.

Construction of the carriage road along this slope was particularly difficult. Blasting was impossible because of the tenuous nature of the rocks, and manually repositioning them proved slow and tedious. At this point it became cost-effective to purchase a steam shovel. In a letter to Rockefeller, Charles Heydt, his assistant in New York, states that "with the use of the shovel, there has actually been completed in one-third of the time, nearly three times as much of the rock-slide work. . . ."

Building a carriage road across the rocky slope is another example of how creative engineering can bridge the gap between man-made structures and natural settings. This massive boulder field

The "tumbledown" was a challenge to the engineers who built this road.

compels the traveler to stop and contemplate the geologic forces that created it and to appreciate the sublime view that the opening provides.

Just beyond the rock slide, another stone bridge was built across Deer Brook.

31

The **Deer Brook Bridge** is the only double-arched span in the system. Somewhat inconspicuous from above, it might be overlooked from a carriage or a fast-moving bicycle. Viewed from below, the imposing double Roman arches are an impressive sight. The bridge was built using dark, old-looking granite that was quarried at the site, allowing the bridge to blend naturally with its surroundings. A round medallion centered in the space between the two arches serves as a datestone. As unique as this is, the original plans called for a bronze deer's head to project from the bridge. Either an objection from the park service or excessive expense prevented this from being done.

The Deer Brook Trail, running from Jordan Pond to Penobscot Mountain, crosses the carriage road at this point. Wherever trails and carriage roads converge, Rockefeller's influence can be seen in creating a natural transition. In this instance, stone steps lead the hiker over the brook to the carriage road and then up into the forest on the side of Sargent Mountain.

Deer Brook Bridge was built of dark, old-looking stone.

DEER BROOK BRIDGE

Bikers stop to enjoy the panorama from the side of Sargent Mountain.

Bear to the left at the next two intersections (both labeled 10), following the "Around the Mountain" signs.

Except for the one leading up Day Mountain, none of the carriage roads actually goes to a mountaintop. Although the most dramatic views are from the summits, Rockefeller clearly wanted to restrict traffic there and thereby preserve the mountain peaks. Nonetheless, the Sargent Mountain section of the road does reach above treeline and provides sweeping vistas to the north and the west.

As the road begins its serpentine climb, it crosses the **Chasm Brook Bridge**. After a heavy spring rain, the brook dramatically plunges fifteen feet over a series of granite steps before entering the chasm and passing beneath the bridge. Built with a low, segmented arch and spiraled end posts, Chasm Brook Bridge contains elements of several previously constructed bridges. Its edges are relatively smooth, but the hand-chiseled rock faces are rough and natural looking, reflecting the jagged walls of the chasm below.

Beyond the bridge, the road climbs to the highest elevation in the carriage-road system: 780 feet. The view opens to a panorama of lakes, islands, and ocean, framed by distant mountains. It is a complex landscape, with bodies of water carving islands of land. Winding along the mountainside, the carriage road intermittently passes through shaded, wooded canyons and sunny, open ledges. Then, from the side of Parkman Mountain, the traveler is presented with a spectacular view of Somes Sound, with Blue Hill in the distance. This vantage point is one of the park's most interesting locations from which to watch the setting sun.

The road traversing Parkman Mountain provides an ideal spot to watch the setting sun.

Hadlock Pond Loop

Alternating granite with red brick created the stripes.

BROWN MOUNTAIN GATE

This section of the carriage road makes a 3.9-mile circuit beginning and ending at the Brown Mountain Gate Lodge on route 198, just north of Northeast Harbor. After leaving the nearby parking area, take a left at intersection 18. In about a mile, you will cross the Hadlock Brook and gradually begin the ascent toward Parkman Mountain.

Like the Jordan Pond Gate Lodge, which was built in the same year, the **Brown Mountain Gate Lodge** was designed to control traffic and to serve as an invitation to the carriage-road system. Located on a hill overlooking Northeast Harbor, this complex is larger than its counterpart at Jordan Pond.

The styles of the two lodges are similar though not identical. Both structures feature striped masonry, but in the Brown Mountain Gate Lodge, alternating granite and red brick creates this effect. The curved wall is broken only at the north end, by the large semi-octagonal towers that frame the massive cypress gate. The intricately carved wooden spindles that adorn many of the windows are an indication of the attention paid to detail.

34

Brown Mountain Gate lodge

Attention to detail is evident throughout the design.

"Landscapes move us in a manner more nearly analogous to the action of music than to anything else.... Gradually and silently the charm overcomes us; we know not exactly where or how."
Frederick Law Olmsted

Although the noted landscape architect Frederick Law Olmsted was not involved with Acadia's carriage roads, he certainly influenced Rockefeller's ideas about landscape design. As a frequent visitor to New York City's Central Park, which Olmsted designed and built in the mid-1800s, Rockefeller admired many of the park's stone structures. Olmsted had pioneered the idea of creating a gentle, natural setting in the midst of a bustling metropolis to provide a contrast and escape for harried city dwellers. By extension, he felt that roadways in a natural environment should present the landscape as a "series of visual experiences." Clearly this is what Rockefeller had in mind when creating Acadia's carriage-road system.

At Rockefeller's request, the **Hadlock Brook Bridge** was modeled after one that crosses a little lake at 59th Street in Central Park. In Acadia, this stone bridge portrays *the* idyllic woodland scene. Surrounded by an open evergreen forest, it gently rises, inviting you to pause at its crest and watch the brook passing through the forest, never drawing attention to itself. The real success of this bridge is that many travelers cross it and admire the landscape but are unaware of the effort that made this scene possible. The carriage roads and bridges were built as reflections of nature's harmony, not as monuments to human engineering.

After leaving the bridge, the road climbs for some distance up the side of Parkman Mountain, presenting views of Upper Hadlock Pond and the ocean beyond.

Bear right at both intersections 13 and 12 as the road follows the contour of the mountainside.

Hadlock Brook Bridge mirrors nature's harmony.

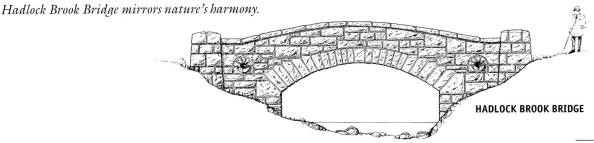

HADLOCK BROOK BRIDGE

The carriage road presents the landscape as a series of visual experiences, including Upper Hadlock Pond.

The final bill exceeded $58,000, more than fifteen times that of the Cobblestone Bridge, built only eight years earlier.

Less than a tenth of a mile up the road, you will encounter the **Waterfall Bridge**, which was built the following year. Construction procedures were modified to reduce the cost overruns that plagued the Hemlock Bridge: winter construction was halted; stones were cut rougher, with larger mortar joints; and a quarry was found nearby. Designers built a model to aid the masons in cutting the granite blocks to size. But the Waterfall Bridge had its own special conditions, and in the end its cost ran 25 percent over the original estimate. At this point Rockefeller hired a superintendent to oversee construction at his estate and on future bridges.

These problems notwithstanding, the bridge clearly contributed to the spectacle of the site. On either side of its skewed arch are buttress-like towers that form viewing platforms at road level. The north wall faces a forty-foot waterfall that is in its full glory when the snow melts in early spring. When first built, the south-facing platforms gave a spectacular view over the Hadlock Ponds to the ocean beyond. Today, however, the view has been blocked as the forest has matured.

A 1929 article in the *Boston Globe* described the reporter's feeling after he hiked to the Waterfall Bridge: "… in graceful arch a bridge crosses a brook. The sound of tumbling white water over the rocks at Waterfall Bridge is in no sense foreign to the lines of the bridge itself, no intruder upon this sylvan scene but fitting the whole in strong and simple lines . . . a fair demonstration that beauty is forgotten toil, for the hand of man has aided, not disturbed the sylvan spots of beauty. "

Beyond the two bridges, the road gradually descends back to the Brown Mountain Gate Lodge. Bear right at intersection 19 then left at 18 to return to the parking area.

From the carriage road, the **Hemlock Bridge** might appear as nothing more than coping stones that line the road on a sharp curve. But viewed from below, it rises from the forest floor as an imposing wall of stone. The structure's massive Gothic arch creates a backdrop for the large hemlock trees that lean across the stream. Small false arches mirror the main arch on each side as the bridge gently curves to follow the hillside.

Problems with construction of the Hemlock Bridge made it one of the most expensive to build. No acceptable quarry could be found at the site, so the stone had to be hauled in at great cost. In an effort to complete the bridge for the spring of 1924, work continued throughout the winter, further slowing construction and increasing costs.

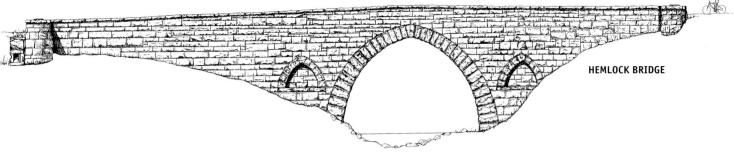

HEMLOCK BRIDGE

Hemlock Bridge rises from the forest floor like an imposing wall of stone.

The skewed arch of Waterfall Bridge frames a forty-foot waterfall.

WATERFALL BRIDGE

The carriage road skirts the edge of Gilmore Meadow.

Water lily

Aunt Betty's Pond

(Route 102 parking area to Eagle Lake)

Beginning at the Parkman Mountain parking area, take a left as you enter the carriage road, which gradually descends for 3.2 miles through a diverse woodland. Just before intersection 11, the road crosses a wet, open meadow. Approach quietly, and watch for wildlife.

Gilmore Meadow is an environment that is neither solid land nor open water. At some point in its past this was a shallow pond, and someday in the future it may become dry land. Until then it fills an intermediate niche that is an ideal home and feeding ground for deer, otter, beaver and any number of birds, reptiles, and amphibians.

During construction of the carriage roads, consideration was given to the idea of damming and flooding the meadow, turning it back into a pond. Paul Simpson argued that the meadow would soon become filled with bushes and trees, thereby losing its beauty. He noted that a pond could provide a source of water to fight potential fires. Both Rockefeller and Farrand felt that "the little meadow is more charming than a lake . . ." so it was left unchanged.

The fear of the meadow's becoming overgrown proved unfounded as beaver activity has periodically flooded it, keeping it in a continual flux between pond and marsh. After examining the meadow, take a left at the intersection, and continue on to Aunt Betty's Pond.

Ponds and lakes are resting places for water as it makes its way from higher ground back to the sea. Many are temporary features with a distinct beginning and end, changing as they age. Upon entering a lake, stream water slows and deposits

Bullfrog

Dragonfly

Pickerel Weed

Cotton Grass

its load of sand, silt, or stone. Over time, these deposits may fill the lake until it becomes dry land. The process of aging comprises a transition from deep open lake to shallow pond then grassy marsh, treed swamp, and finally to forest. The stages may be halting and uneven, but the end result is inevitable.

Aunt Betty's Pond is in the final stages of its existence, as vegetation rapidly encroaches on the last remaining open water. Ironically, the overabundance of life here is causing its demise. Ponds, marshes, and swamps are incredibly rich environments. Warm, shallow, nutrient-rich water provides the ideal habitat for grasses, sedges, flowers, and shrubs. Attracted by this vegetation is an equally diverse profusion of animal life, from microscopic organisms to insects, fish, reptiles, amphibians, birds, and mammals. The greater the abundance of such life, the faster organic matter accumulates, and the sooner the pond fills and ceases to be. Organisms rush toward the future, changing their environment into one where they are not welcome. Eventually Aunt Betty's Pond will become what Gilmore Meadow is today.

The red-spotted newt is the animal equivalent of the aging pond. In its lifetime, the newt goes through a dramatic transformation from an aquatic larva to a colorful, terrestrial red "eft."

Gilmore Meadow is an open, wet, and grassy marsh.

Aunt Betty's Pond is slowly becoming a meadow.

A ring-necked snake

A red eft—the terrestrial stage of the red-spotted newt.

The eft finds protection from the sun under logs and rocks, but after a rain it will often be seen boldly walking the forest floor in search of food. After two to three years on land, it returns to the water, where it becomes a fully mature adult. Hundreds of such stories could be told about the diverse life-forms that make this pond their home.

The carriage road beyond Aunt Betty's Pond makes a long, rather steep ascent to a rocky out-crop with a view of Acadia's mountains and Eagle Lake below. A gradual descent, through an open evergreen forest, ends at intersection 9, where taking a left will bring you to Eagle Lake Bridge and Route 233.

Eagle Lake

Beginning at the Eagle Lake parking area on route 233, pass beneath the stone bridge (intersection 6), and proceed around the lake in either direction. Turn toward the lake at each intersection along the way, and the circular route will return you to the parking lot in 5.8 miles.

S top beneath the lancet arch of the **Eagle Lake Bridge** for a close look at the granite blocks lining its barrel vault. Notice that the stones on the north side, away from the lake, show less weathering and no signs of calcium carbonate formation. (Deposits often form on the bridges as this mineral is leached from the mortar used to bond the stones.) The explanation for this incongruity stretches over forty-eight years (1926–1974).

The bridge was built in 1928 to help carriage travelers safely avoid a motor road (now Route 233). It was decided that the carriage road would pass beneath the paved road in what George Dorr called a "tunnel." Because this bridge would carry heavier loads from the automobile traffic, it was constructed with a thicker road cushion, and design modifications gave the surface layer a full twenty-one feet of width. The tunnel beneath features an ample sixteen-foot clearance to allow adequate headroom for passengers in open coaches.

When the plan was presented to the town of Bar Harbor in 1926, it was suggested that the width be increased to twenty-seven feet to accommodate future automobile traffic. This proposal was rejected by Rockefeller because of the added $4,000 expense. He noted that since "the bridge onto the island is only twenty feet wide, it stands to reason that there is no possible ground for urging that this bridge be made wider than twenty-one feet." This was uncharacteristic of Rockefeller, who usually considered problems that could be more expensive to correct in the future.

The cost of building the bridge in 1927–1928 was in excess of $67,500. In 1974 the structure was, in

Eagle Lake Bridge was referred to as the "tunnel" by early park superintendent George B. Dorr.

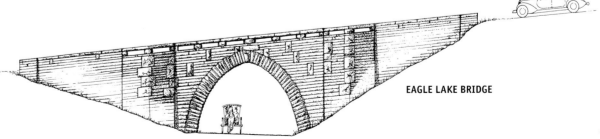

EAGLE LAKE BRIDGE

Though once slated for recreational development Eagle Lake has been preserved in its natural state.

needles growing in that direction, so the branches that developed faced away from the lake, changing forever the shape of these trees.

The pines were already large when the carriage road was built at their feet. It provided access to firefighters during the horrendous blaze of 1947, which may have saved these trees from the fate of nearly all the others in the path of the flames. Now, in old age, the twisted pines stand in defiance of the wind and the weather. Their unique shapes catch the attention of those walking the carriage road, and their exposed roots provide benches upon which travelers can sit and view the pond.

In the shelter of their branches are young pines that may someday grow to take their place as the dominant trees at the edge of the lake.

fact, expanded to accommodate a wider motor road. According to Keith Miller, then superintendent of the park, most contractors who bid on the project planned to dismantle the north wall and number each stone, then rebuild it according to the new specifications. Their bids were exorbitantly high.

A local contractor, Harold MacQuinn, proposed another method to solve the problem. He would separate the north wall, place it on ball bearings and slide it thirteen feet. The space created would then be filled using the same type of granite as in the original Eagle Lake Bridge. The estimate was considered reasonable: $350,000. MacQuinn received the bid and also an award from the Federal Highway Administration for devising this unique solution. The stones that line the barrel of the arch now reflect both phases of the bridge's construction. Although the stonework is the same, the weathering and mineral deposits clearly distinguish which part was built in 1928 and which in 1974.

Today the bridge also serves as an entrance to the carriage-road routes around Eagle Lake and Witch Hole Pond. The original plans for this area called for the construction of a large teahouse and riding stable on the shore of Eagle Lake, but the idea was abandoned because of the fear that this might jeopardize the quality of the water in the lake, which serves as the water supply for the town of Bar Harbor.

Along the shore of Eagle Lake are large, isolated white pines that dwarf the smaller trees around them and may be well over two hundred years old. Their position between the lake and the carriage road has directed their growth and also been their salvation. Maybe because they were near the water's edge during the lumbering years of the 1800s, these trees were spared the ax. As they grew taller and broader, however, the open lake began to assert its influence. The cold winter wind blowing off the ice killed any new

Having weathered storms and fires, these old pines now dominate the landscape.

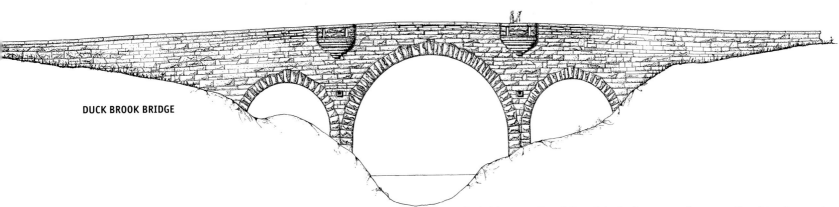

DUCK BROOK BRIDGE

The bridge over Duck Brook is the largest and most refined in the carriage-road system.

Witch Hole Pond

The Witch Hole Pond section can be reached from a number of different locations: Eagle Lake (6); the Visitor Center parking area; or Duck Brook Bridge (5), off the New Eagle Lake Road. Although parking is limited at the Duck Brook entrance, this tour will begin there for the sake of continuity.

Duck Brook Bridge is the largest, most expensive, and most refined bridge in the system. It is one of only two with a triple arch, Stanley Brook being the other. Although Rockefeller did not want his structures to dominate the landscape, the Duck Brook Bridge demands to be considered. The twenty-foot-wide roadway is dressed on both sides with squared capstones and horizontal openings clustered above each arch. Four cantilevered balconies provide views out to Frenchman Bay and upstream, into the woods. A stone stairway traverses the south wall of the bridge, providing access to the brook below. From nearly any vantage, Duck Brook Bridge has a commanding presence, yet it does not appear foreign to the site.

The nature of this bridge seems to be an exception to Rockefeller's ideal—that the carriage-road bridges be rustic and relatively unadorned. It has

An active beaver lodge at Witch Hole Pond.

The scarlet leaves of swamp maples light up Witch Hole Pond in autumn.

been suggested that the refinement of the Duck Brook Bridge may have been a reaction to the controversy over the Bubble Pond Bridge, where the architect's designs were rejected by the park service. Like most of the other bridge sites, Duck Brook was on Rockefeller land, so no such approval was required. This allowed the designer free rein, and the result was this grand structure.

Bear left after crossing the bridge (5). Within a mile, you will come to an intersection (4). Continue straight for another mile, at which point Witch Hole Pond will appear on your right.

In the fall of 1947, dry conditions and high winds fanned a fire that burned more than seventeen thousand acres on Mount Desert Island. The damage was considerable, including the loss of five lives and the destruction of many homes, hotels, and large summer cottages. The flames

brought to a close an era of elegance in and around Bar Harbor. For the forest, the fire was both an end and a beginning: It ended the dominance of evergreens on the island and began a period where broad-leaved trees would share the landscape. Where the fire burned, the destruction of the spruce/fir forest was nearly complete. Charred tree stumps can still be seen nearly everywhere in this area, as **Witch Hole Pond** was in the direct line of the fire.

Plants recover slowly in this cold northern environment, but by the following spring, saplings of birch, beech, aspen, and oak were already emerging from the ashes. This new forest soon changed the tempo of life on the island. Deciduous trees, on the whole, are more useful to wildlife species. Their leaves, bark, and fruit create a diverse selection of edible foods. The deer population increased, bird species shifted, and beaver communities thrived. Nearly every pond and lake on the island has at one time or another supported a colony of beavers, whose appetite for deciduous

trees is insatiable. When the food supply at one pond becomes inadequate, they simply find or create another. Beaver activity may slow the succession of plant communities, but in time the cycle of life will come full circle, and the conifers will once again reign as kings of Acadia's forest.

At the northern end of Witch Hole Pond, the carriage road makes a 1.6-mile loop over **Paradise Hill**. Rockefeller considered this section to be the "Grand Northern terminus," and from its rocky crest he provided sweeping vistas of Hulls Cove and Frenchman Bay, with Beatrix Farrand giving special care to adjacent plantings. A discerning eye may also discover the remnants of an old carriage path, now overgrown with trees, that at one time may have led to a cottage with a spectacular view.

The end of this section of road (3) intersects with the Witch Hole Pond road leading back to Duck Brook Bridge, completing the loop.

Paradise Hill is known as "the Grand Northern terminus."

An Enduring Gift

Acadia's carriage-road system is truly a national treasure. It epitomizes the American spirit of preservation and philanthropy that prevailed in the early twentieth century. This vision of John D. Rockefeller Jr. combines the artistry and skills of the architects, engineers, masons, and laborers who converged on Mount Desert Island from 1913 through 1940. Today, the roads serve as reminders of a slower and gentler time, when a carriage ride through the forests and hills of Mount Desert Island was an adventure of discovery. This man-made structure in the midst of a national park also serves as a message to future generations, showing them how an understanding of the land combined with creative engineering can permit us to interact with nature with a gentle hand.

The carriage roads have brought us into the heart of the national park only to reveal that there is still more. Rising above the wooded roads are the exposed granite summits from which the island got its name, but they are a topic for another time.

Fall colors enhance the enjoyment of a walk on the carriage roads.

The Waterfall Bridge provides a platform from which to enjoy the cataract.

Outcroppings of lichen-encrusted granite appear at nearly every bend.

46

Fallen leaves turn the carriage road into a colorful mosaic.

Where to find the Stone Bridges of the Carriage Road System

Summary of Bridge Characteristics

(Note: The bridges listed here are only those associated with the carriage-road system. Others may be encountered throughout the park.)

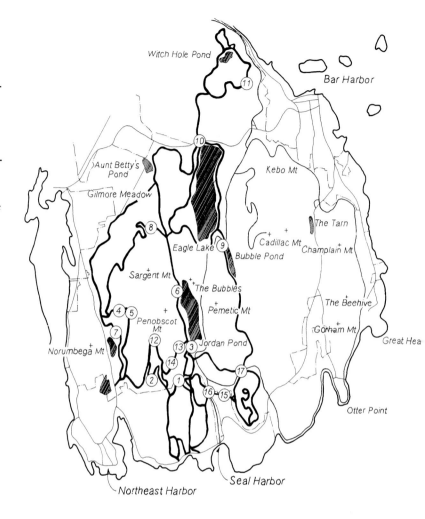

Name	Date	Length	Height	Comments
1 Cobblestone	1917	150'	21'	only bridge made entirely with cobblestones
2 Little Harbor Brook	1919	41.5'	10.3'	
3 Jordan Pond Dam	1920	41.5'	10.4'	same design as the Little Harbor Brook Bridge
4 Hemlock	1924	200'	35.5'	built during the winter at great expense
5 Waterfall	1925	120'	31'	skewed arch
6 Deer Brook	1925	78'	22.4'	double-arched, dark, old-looking stone
7 Hadlock Brook	1926	46.9'	12.8'	modeled after a bridge in Central Park (N.Y.)
8 Chasm Brook	1926	54'	25'	built 600' above sea level
9 Bubble Pond	1928	75'	20'	only solid stone masonry bridge
10 Eagle Lake*	1928	118'	24'	widened in 1974
11 Duck Brook	1929	207'	43'	most expensive—$77,837
12 Amphitheater	1931	245'	27'	longest bridge
13 West Branch	1931	115'	22'	narrow 6'-wide arch
14 Cliffside	1932	250'	29'	crenellated parapet
15 Jordan Pond Road	1932	85'	19.5'	may still have Beatrix Farrand plantings
16 Stanley Brook	1933	180'	23.5'	restored in 2001
17 Triad-Day Mountain	1941	74.5'	20.5'	built by the National Park Service

* The Eagle Lake Bridge does not have a date stone.

References

Abrell, Diana. *A Pocket Guide to the Carriage Roads of Acadia National Park.* Camden: Down East Books, 1995.

Gilman, Richard A. *The Geology of Mount Desert Island, A Visitor's Guide to the Geology of Acadia National Park.* Augusta: Maine Geological Survey, Department of Conservation, 1988.

Haynes, Steven. Local historian; conversation with the author. Mount Desert Island, 2001.

Layton, Victor. "Mount Desert Island's Granite Heritage." Camden: *Down East*, June 1982.

Miller, Keith. Superintendent of Acadia National Park from 1971 to 1978; conversation with the author. Mount Desert Island, 2001.

Olsen, W. Kent. President, Friends of Acadia; conversation with the author. Mount Desert Island, 2001.

Rieley, William D. and Roxanne S. Brouse. *Historic Resource Study for the Carriage Road System, Acadia National Park.* Charlottesville: Rieley & Associates, 1989.

Roberts, Ann Rockefeller, *Mr. Rockefeller's Roads, the Untold Story of Acadia's Carriage Roads & Their Creator.* Camden: Down East Books, 1990.

Rockefeller, John D. Jr. Web site: www.rockefeller.edu/archive.ctr/jdrjrbio.html

Sharpe, Grant and Wenonah Grant. *101 Wildflowers of Acadia National Park.* Seattle: University of Washington Press, 1977.

Smythe, Herbert Weir. "Automobiles—The Mount Desert Town Meeting." Bar Harbor: *Bar Harbor Life*, August 1913.

Vanasse, Hangen, Brustlin, Inc./McGinley Hart & Associates. *Historic Bridge Reconnaissance Survey, Carriage Road System, Acadia National Park.* Bar Harbor: National Park Service, 1994